This Book Belongs To:

____

SHEBA BLAKE PUBLISHING CORP.
WWW.SHEBABLAKE.COM

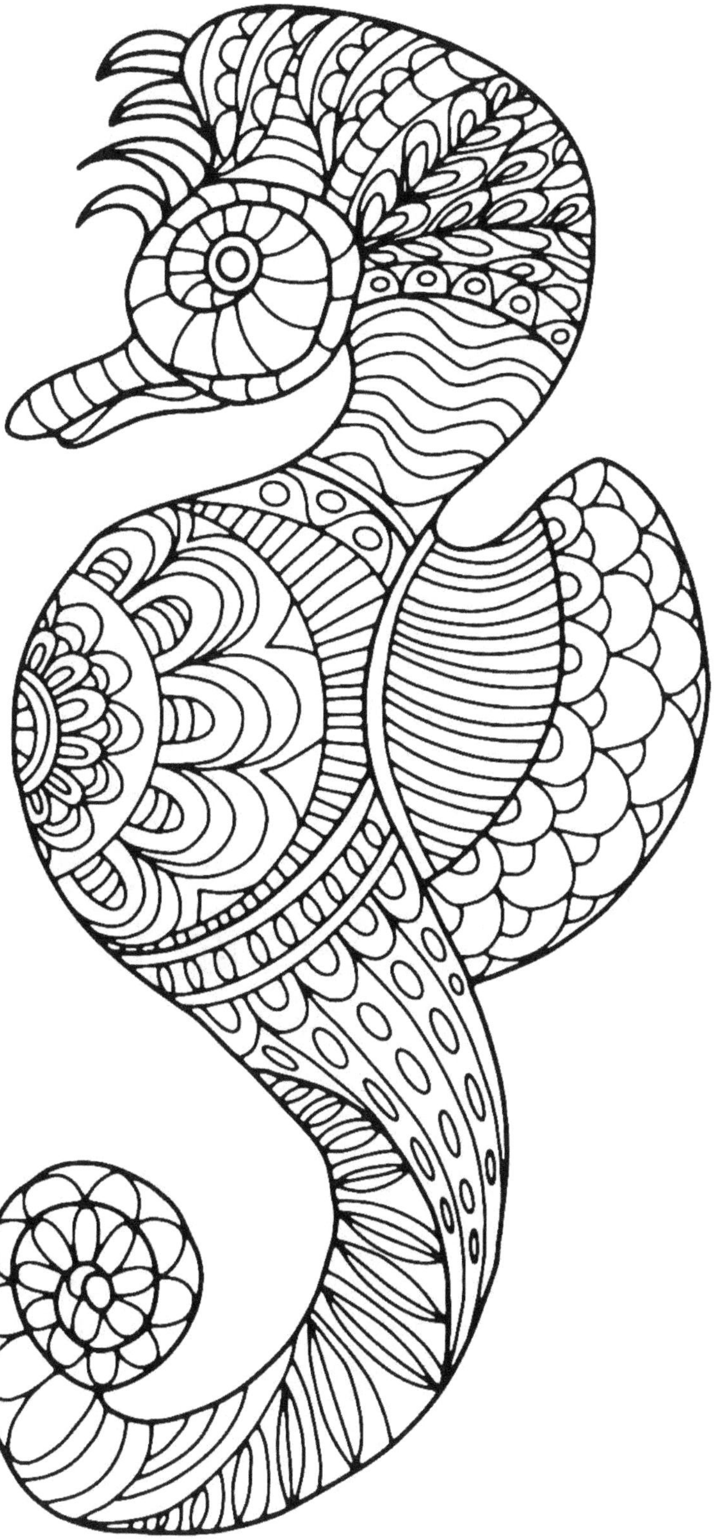

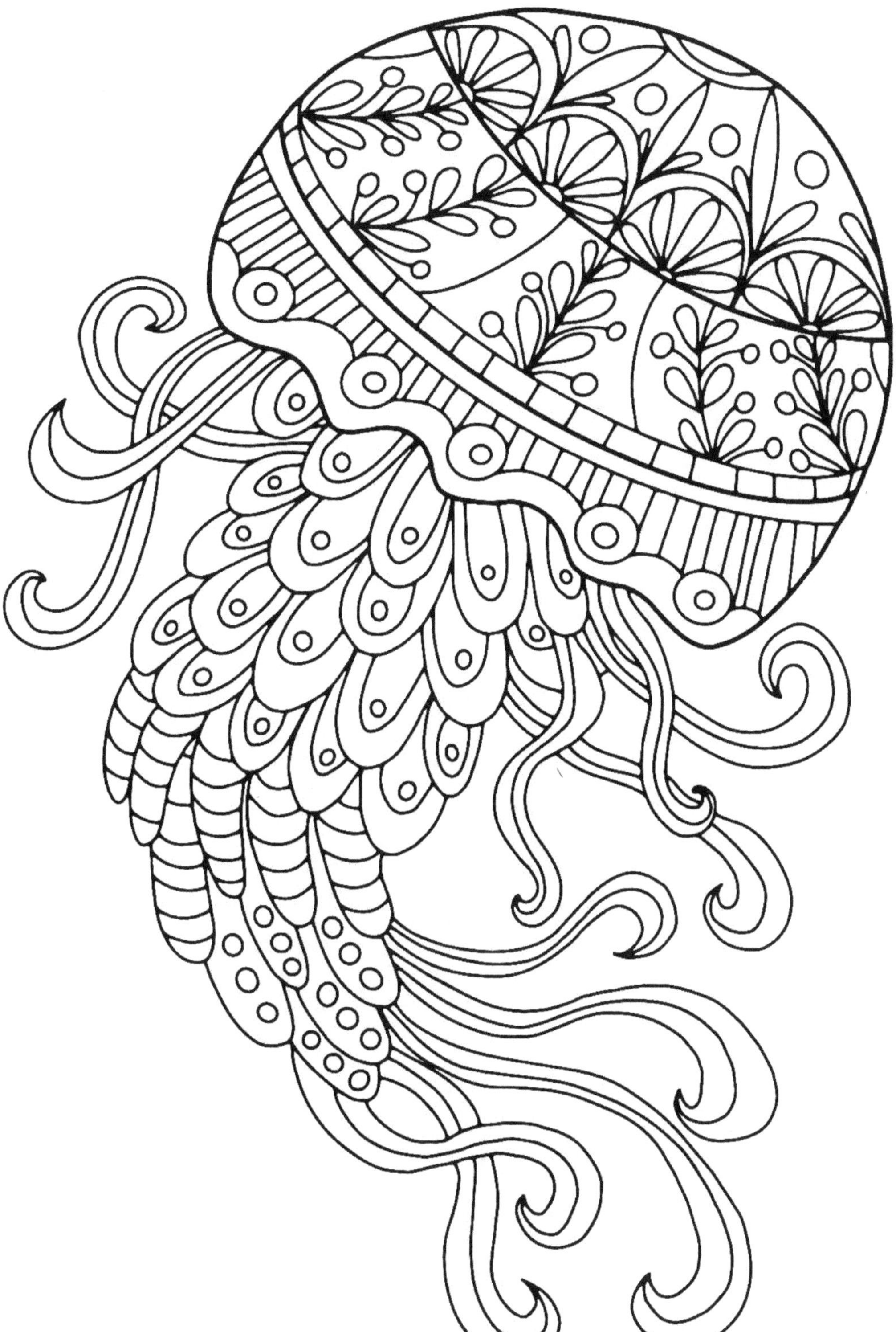

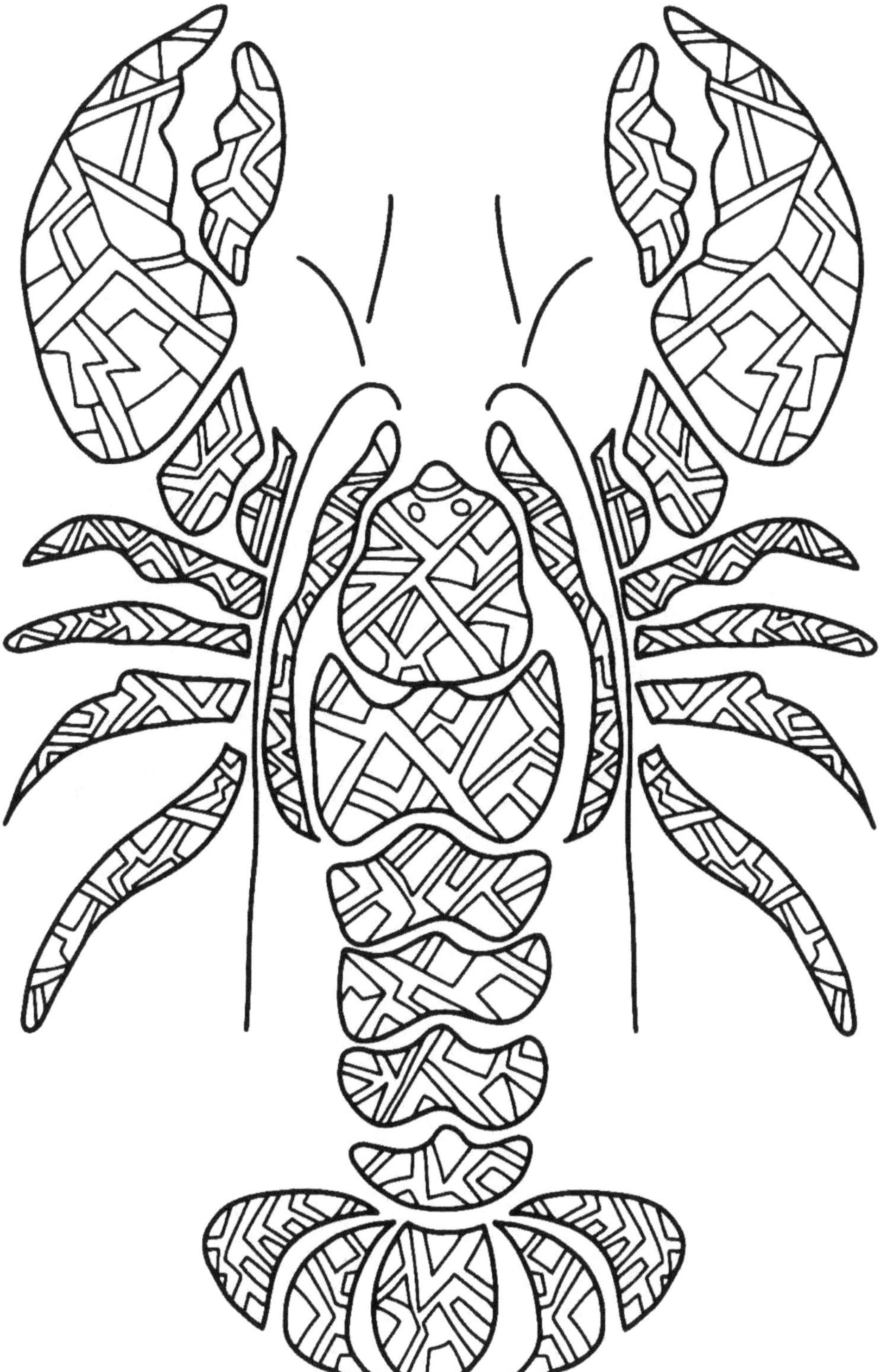

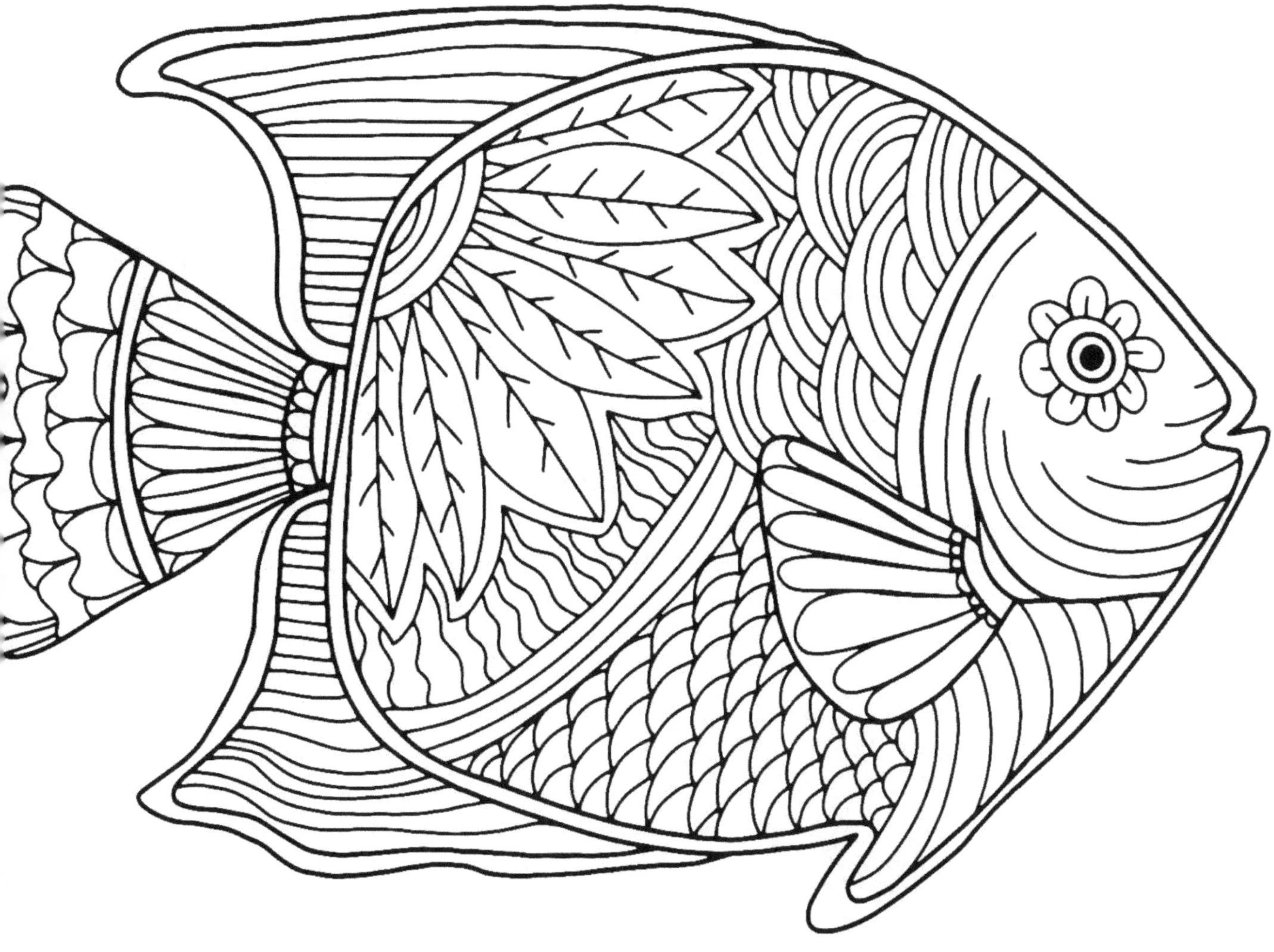

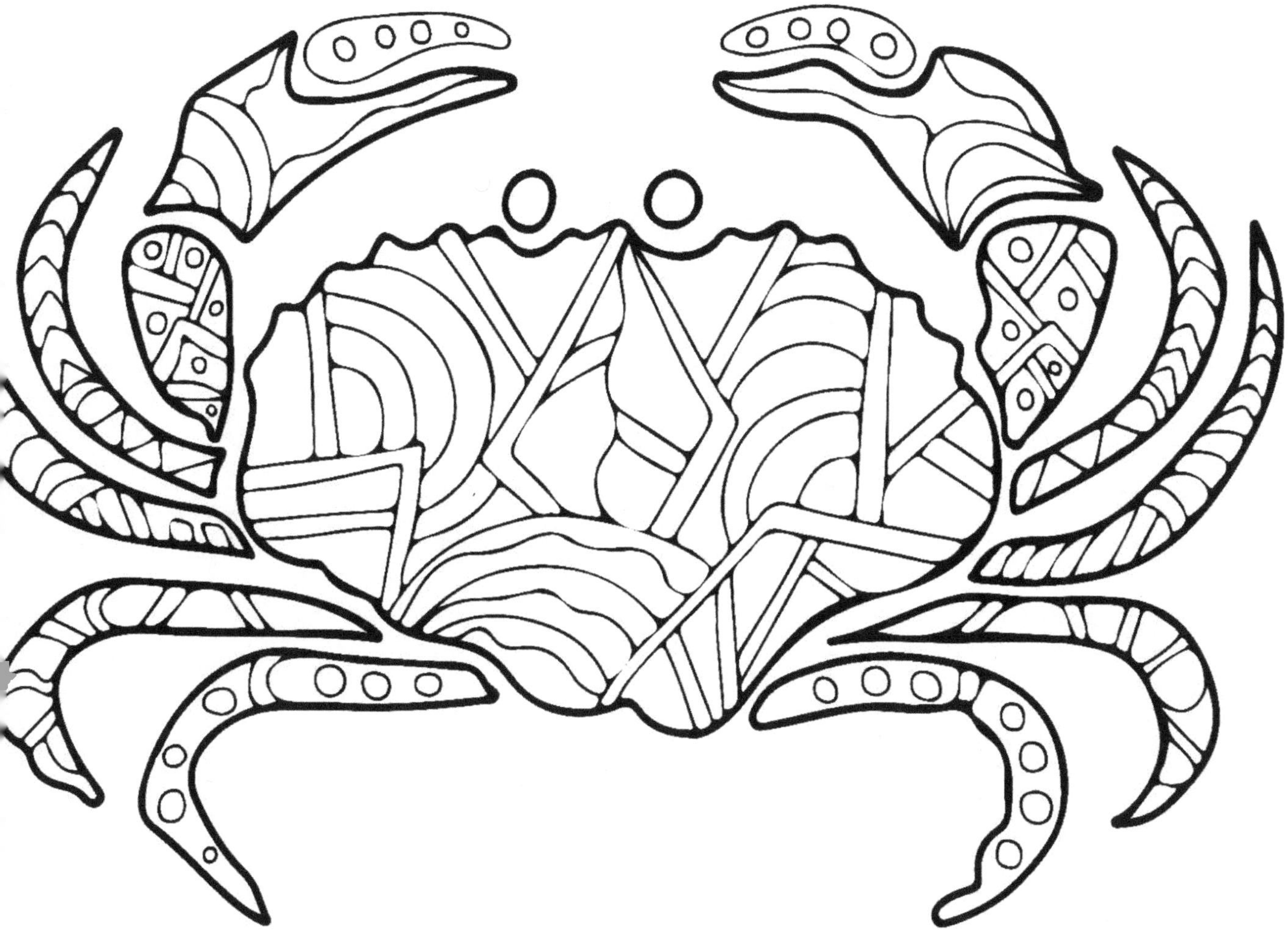

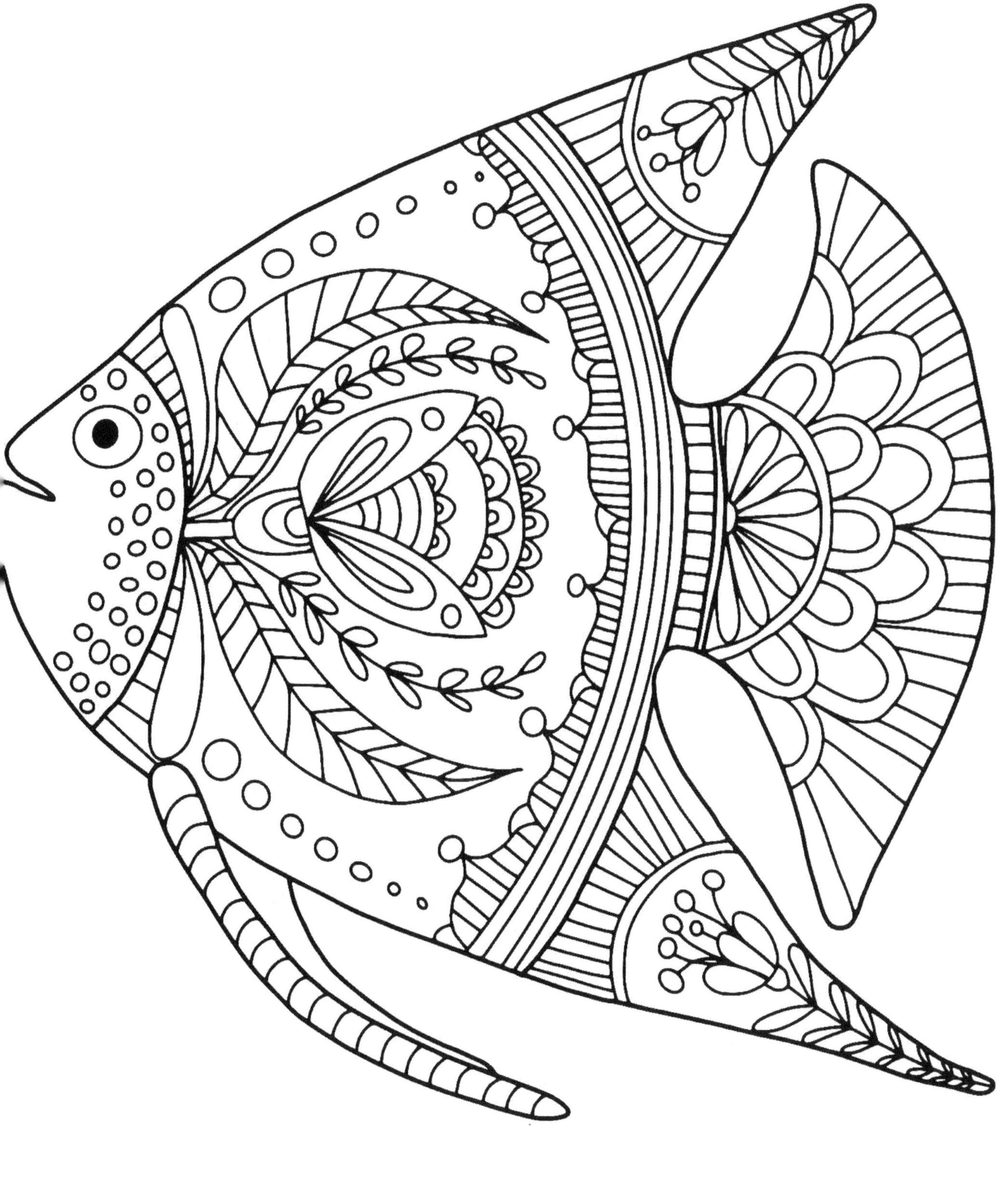

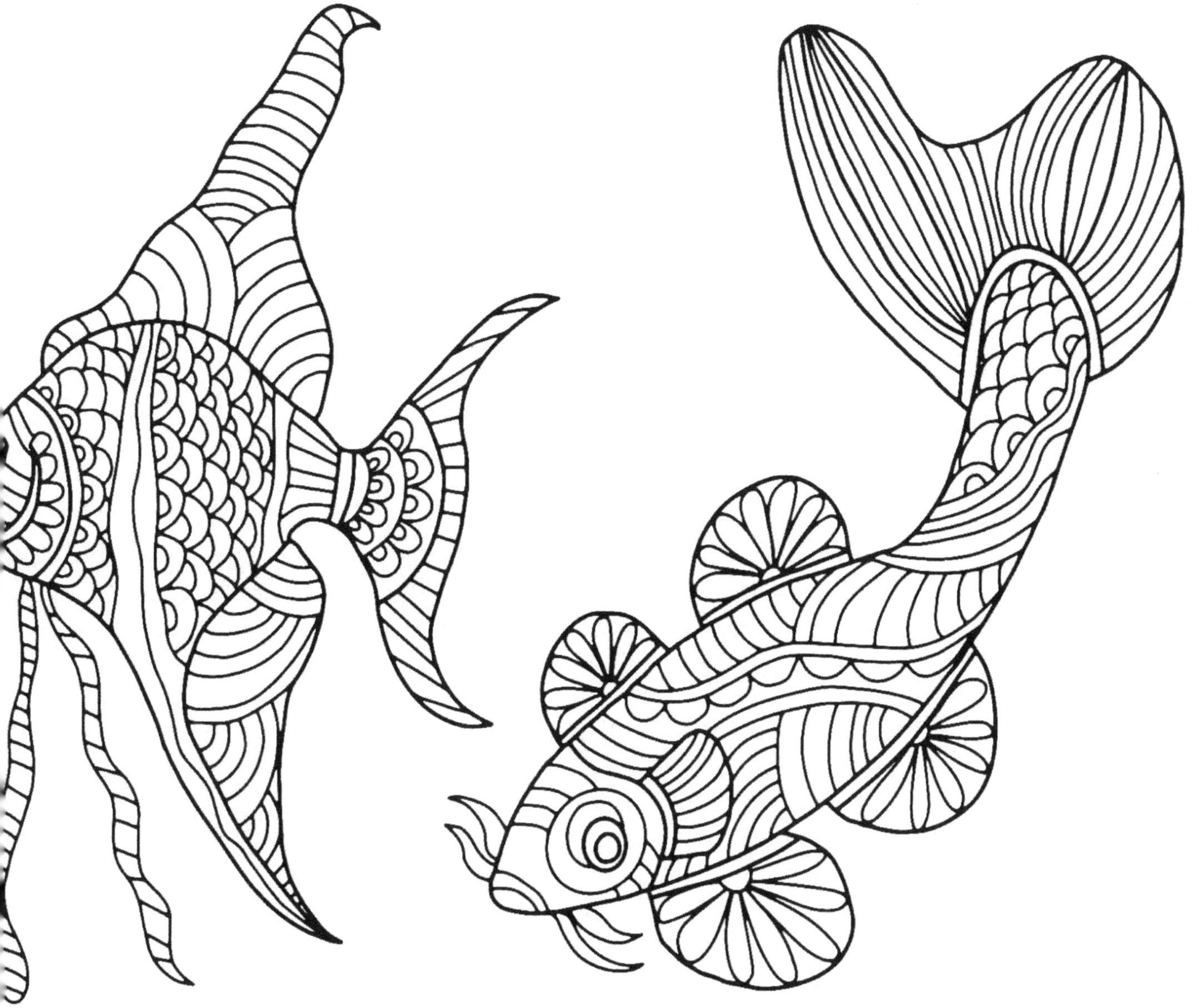

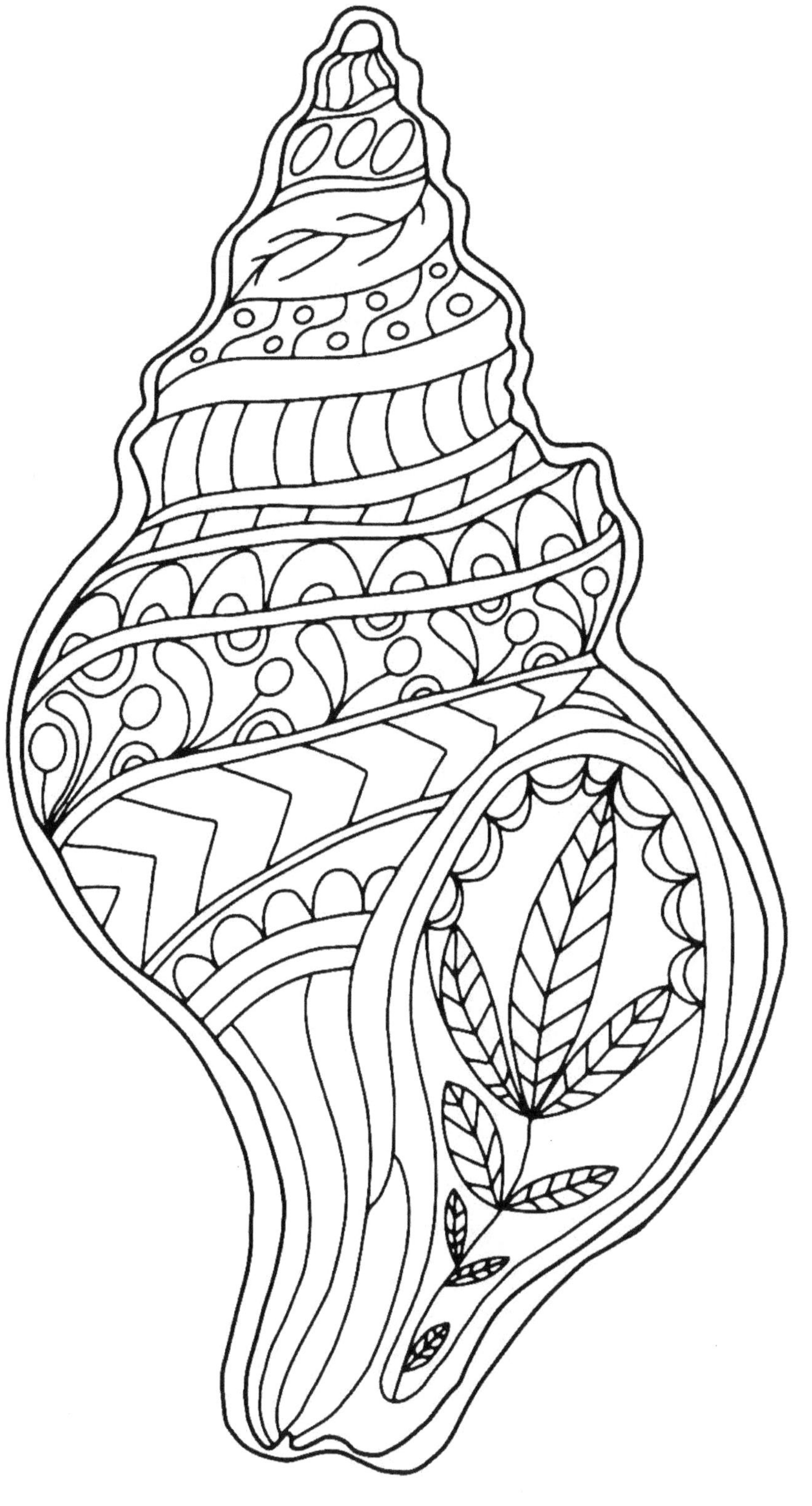

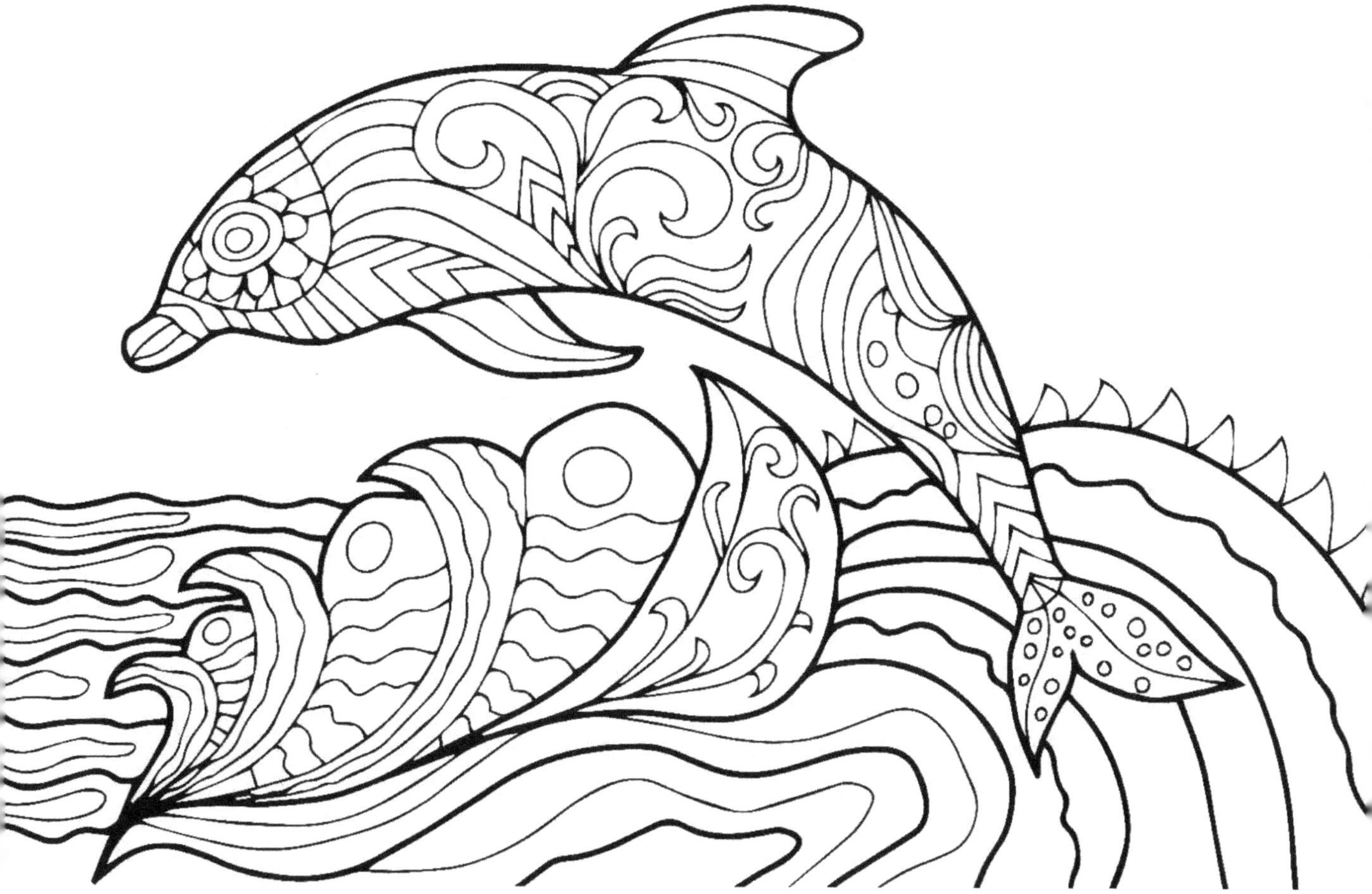

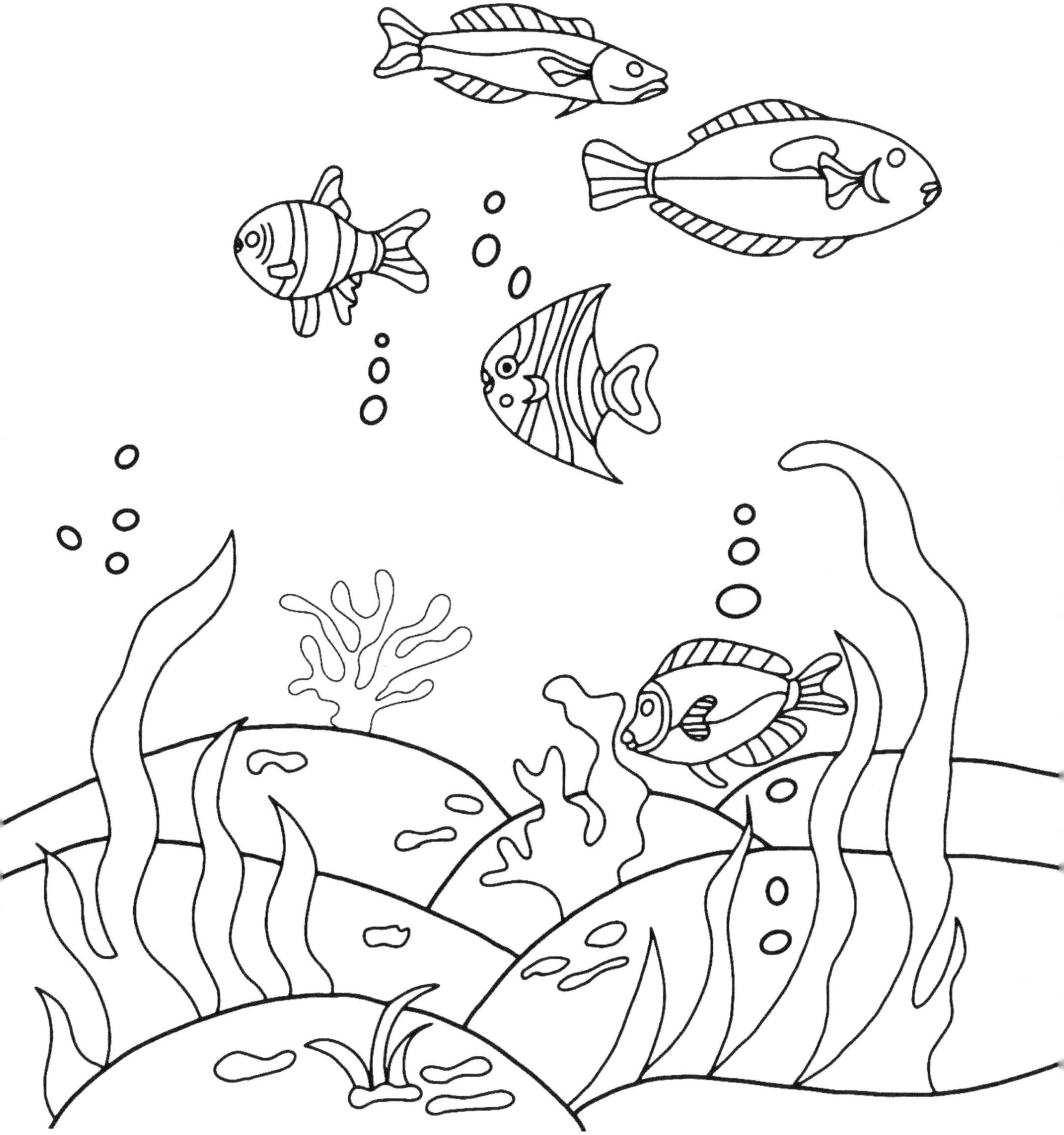

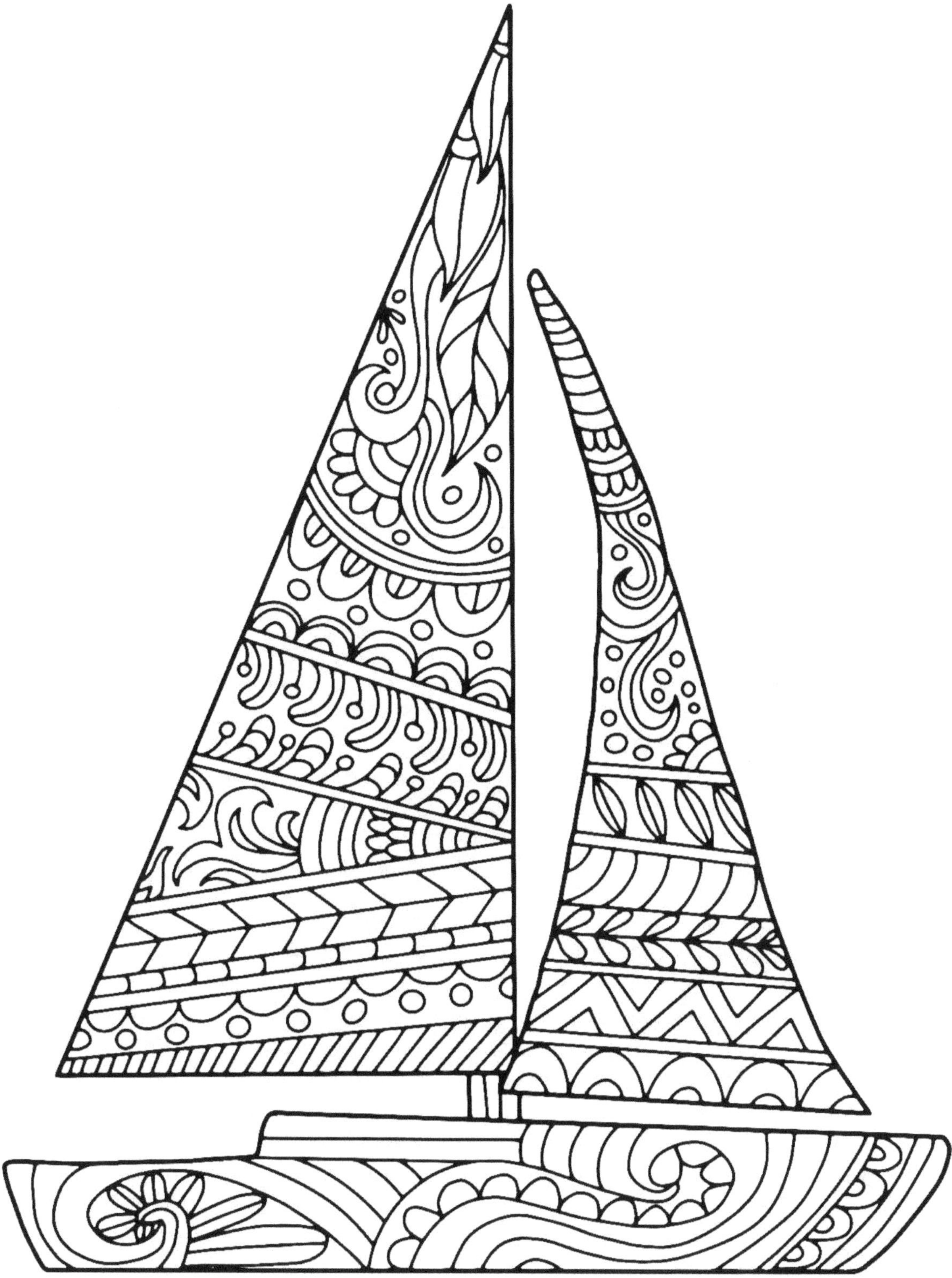

CPSIA information can be obtained
at www.ICGtesting.com
Printed in the USA
LVHW062226280221
679631LV00047BB/786

9 781222 301274